HAPPY BIRTHDAY

He could feel it but did not want it to be true. One of his eyes told him it was time to get up, and the other was fighting for him to stay asleep. He hated the mornings. He was so comfortable nestled in the bed, feeling well rested yet wanting to sleep more. The grand life of a teenager, he thought. But then he remembered what today was as his eyes began working in tandem.

Finn had been looking forward to an exciting eighteenth birthday. He knew that turning eighteen would give him a new sense of freedom that he had been wanting. He was intent on having the power to make adult decisions and was tired of hearing others tell him, "You are too young, Finn." and "You will understand when you get older." Finn wondered how many times those phrases were uttered through multiple generations and who started them. He knew, though, there was a lot of truth in them for sure. Finn knew he did not have all the answers and turning eighteen would not give him some new way to solve what lies ahead. Today, he had a great sense of finally becoming that person he was in control of creating. His first thought today was, "Do I get out of bed to enjoy this day or maybe just a little more sleep before I revel in my celebration." He knew he would make many mistakes in his life but was sure that he would learn from them. At least if he did make some mistakes, he was the one in control.

One thing he wanted most was the ability to make decisions that would make a difference not only for him but also for others as well. Finn was the kid that could make friends with strangers. He was well liked in school, and his friends seemed to light up when he was around. Finn thought of his older brother Garrett. He wondered how he had gotten so knowledgeable, and if the errors he made along the way contributed to his ability to understand life and be so successful. Finn felt lucky to have a brother so loving even with so many years between them. He knew he could get guidance and advice when he needed it. His brother would always say, "I know this sounds cliché, but you will learn from your mistakes, trust me. I have made many and see how smart you think I am!"

Finn's parents gave him the room to make decisions but always intervened to help him make him a better choice. While Finn disliked that, he had to agree that they were right and had his best interest in mind. He had close relationships with most of his classmates and noticed that those students who seemed to have discipline issues and those who just struggled to transition through their teens had a common request. They felt that they had unclear boundaries and direction in life. Many admitted to him that while they disliked the parental interactions when given vague direction and no limitations, it often led them to make decisions that would lead them to outcomes that caused stress and even extreme consequences. Finn, too, hated it when his family imposed guidance and rules on him, but when he had the chance to reflect, he felt lucky to have been given the exact boundaries he needed. He knew that those that struggled had no clear stopping point that they wished they were given. Even when their parents threatened consequences, they rarely saw them through, and before long, his classmates knew they were just empty threats, so they went on a less than desirable path. His parents were very consistent in their words. If they imposed a consequence, they stuck to it. He found it so ironic that while he hated these interactions when he was younger, they helped mold him into the person he is today, and now felt appreciative. He was not about to admit to his parents at this point. Maybe when he felt older and wiser, he would, but he would just take it day by day for now.

Finn thought it was now or never to get started on this day of celebrating. How could anyone celebrate his momentous day with him when he would not get out of bed? He made his way downstairs, eager to be basked in love from his parents as he marked his transition to adulthood. He could smell the bacon and knew Mom was making his favorites. Finn could not wait to dig into a stack of blueberry pancakes smothered in butter and syrup. What was it about that smell of bacon that made him feel all comfy? Finn remembered Garrett saying something similar when he would come home on Sunday and could smell the pot roast cooking. He would always comment on how that scent of his favorites just made him feel all warm and fuzzy. Finn thought maybe it was that the smells reminded them of a family being together and sharing meals, which led to that wonderful feeling. Or was it that he and his brother were extreme carnivores, and the smell of meat cooking made them happy? Out of the blue, his mind shifted on that thought to his vegan friends. What foods brought them that same joy? Tofu, beans, nuts, veggies, rice? None of those made any sense. He would have to make a point to ask one of them to see as it puzzled him now. He wondered why he had even thought about it. His mind was always so curious. It felt like it never could be turned off. It seemed he was always thinking about why things happened in specific ways or why people said what they did. Everyone always told him it was just how smart he was. But sometimes he just wanted to think about nothing and have a way for his mind to be quiet and rested.

He made his way briskly to the kitchen to let the celebrating begin. He saw his Mom and greeted her with an animated good morning!

She said, "Happy Birthday, son," pecked him on the cheek and continued to pour another batch of pancakes.

His first thought was, "What the heck?" this was not what he was accustomed to, especially on such an essential day to him. Finn knew his Mom, and he knew this was not the typical emotional, celebratory response he had been expecting. His Mom always gave in to her emotional side, and even little things set off a flow of tears when she was sharing her love. Maybe he was expecting too much. It was such a critical time for him, but perhaps she did not see it the same way. He saw his Dad watching the morning update in the next room, so he thought he would try his luck there.

"Hey, son! Happy Birthday!"

His Dad gave him a big hug and spun back around as if he did not want to miss a second of the morning news. He knew how loved he was, but it still hurt him on the inside as it was not the response he had imagined receiving. Was this it? Is this the feeling of now being an adult? He knew that was not it but could not pinpoint why it seemed so different from his expectations. Finn was having trouble understanding what to do with his emotions. He did not want to be ungrateful, but he did not understand this whole scenario playing out. It felt so disconnected to him.

Finn made his way to the den to grab his books for school. His phone buzzed, and he saw it was his brother Garrett. "Hey, Garrett! What's up?

"Your age, little brother! Happy Birthday! Are you super excited for this next rite of passage in your life?" Finally, Finn thought, someone that gets it.

"Yeah, Garrett, I am. I really want this day to be the beginning of something new for me. I feel like it is a milestone that I need to embrace and do something with."

Garrett told him, "Finn, there is nothing you can't do. There is so much you have already done with your life, and I know your future will be incredible for you. You are a true leader in school, helping with your volunteer efforts, and I know Mom and Dad are so grateful for everything you do to help them and others out."

"Garrett, I am not sure what is going on with Mom and Dad."
They are OK, but I guess I was maybe just expecting something
different for today."

Garrett laughed a bit and said, "Well, Finn, the whole world
was expecting something a much different today." I think what you
see is something many are experiencing today, which is just pure
shock and disbelief."

"About what? Finn asked"

"Mom and Dad are just in disbelief that Baby Frump won the
election."

"Whoa!" "Are you serious, Garrett?"

"Yes, Finn." I am having a hard time understanding it myself.
Dad said that Mom cried herself to sleep last night; she was so
distraught over it."

Finn was beginning to see why his parents were acting as
they did. It really was a shock that they did not expect or want any
part of. He did not think much about it over the past few months
because he always heard the conversations his parents were having
about how there was no way the country could believe in someone
who acted as Frump did. He remembered how comfortable his
parents felt that Sillary would win. Now, Finn was feeling that same
sense of disbelief.

"But Garrett, you mean that the majority of this country
elected someone like that to the office of President? I mean, I get it
now why Mom and Dad are a bit disconnected. How did something
like this happen in this country?" What does this say about us if this
is what everyone thinks is the best choice for one of the most
significant leadership roles in the world? This is the man that talked
about doing things to women that I can't even believe were said. ! I
mean, I am eighteen and should be full of vulgarity and even
offensive to some, but an adult like him acting this way makes me
embarrassed, yet the whole country is good with it?"

" I can see you have as much shock as Mom and Dad."

" I really do! I just don't see why so many thought this was the best choice. I was sure the voters would have made a different choice."

"Well, Finn, you are thinking of the popular vote." You have to think of the Electoral College." "Baby Frump lost the popular vote to Sillary by millions."

"OK, yes, we learned about this in school. I remember that candidates can win even if they do not get the majority of the popular vote. I guess I need a refresh on what I should have been paying attention to in the American History class. What I can't remember is why that happens."

"You are not alone, Finn, it can be confusing, and it can change based on population numbers in states. The electoral vote is determined by the popular vote results within each county. Even though Baby Frump lost most of the popular vote as a whole, he was able to pick up electoral votes based on the states he was able to win. A president can even be elected by only winning 1/5th of the states as long as they gain those with the most electoral votes. Prior presidents have also won the office without gaining the popular vote. That is why completing the Census is so important and why it affects the Electoral College. Population numbers drive how it is allocated. Remember when I was a Census taker a few years back? It was so shocking how many were apathetic to the whole situation. If they really understood how the Census and the Electoral College map are connected it may be different."

"OK, it is starting to come back to me. So, the midterm elections are truly a popular vote where if we do not like how elected officials are conducting themselves, that is our chance to let them know?"

"Yes, Finn, excellent. You did pay attention. The midterm elections are local ones that are strictly driven by the popular votes."

"So my question for the presidential election is, "Does my vote count if the Electoral College determines it?

"Yes, yes, yes, Finn! This is why there are many campaigns you see that have the message to "Get Out and Vote" and "Your Vote Matters." The more votes that are cast increase the popular vote and lead to the way the Electoral College goes. If people stay home, then their intent is not shown about what they want, leading the Electoral College to cast a ballot for those who expressed the choice they wanted."

"I guess this means there are still millions of people in this country that voted for him and thought he would do what? I do not see what people think he will do."

"Well, he made people believe he is the one who is going to make changes they want to see. We have to see how that plays out, but some voters feel threatened by the changes in society toward race; some are looking for economic optimism, and some believe he will change how things move in the world of politics. No one knows how it will unfold, and so many voted for him even if they cannot stand his actions just to see the change they are hoping for."

"So, in many ways, it is not like they support what he says just that they support the need for a change that aligns with what they want?"

"Exactly, Finn,"

"It makes a bit more sense when you think about the reasoning. It is still so shocking; I guess because it is just not what seemed like the normal result I would expect."

"I think normal is going to change for all of us, Finn. Baby Frump has already demonstrated he does not adhere to established norms. A lot of that is why he was elected. People are looking for dramatic change, and many see his unabashed approach as the way to do it. I think that his supporters will see that come to light as things move forward. He is exposed to the world at this point, and what he says matters tremendously. He will have to either step up or decide which path he will take. There are only so many out there that may be willing to not only accept his words and actions but also who are also willing to support him to move his agenda forward."

"Wow, bro, I do not know how you always have the right answers, but I appreciate you and your grasp of the world. I hope I can one day have the potential that you have."

"You already do, brother. It is all about how you choose to use it and how to make it meaningful. Over time, you will see that each day something you come across gives you unique insights into the world, and you will choose how to use those to make a difference. No one can take away your passion for learning and wanting to do your best. Every bit of knowledge you gain gives you the power to make a difference for yourself and others."

"Thanks, Garrett, you always make a difference for me, and I admire you. I think breakfast is ready, so I better go. I will see you tonight at dinner."

"See you later, Finn. Make it a great birthday, and make today your mission to see how you can change the world!"

CONVERSATIONS

     Finn was eager to head to school and see the reaction of his classmates. His school held a mock election, and it was overwhelmingly in favor of Sillary winning. He wondered what they would think of the results. He saw Kyle and Kendra having a conversation that he knew had voted for different candidates. He could not wait to join in.

"Hey guys, anything new today?"

"Well, yes, Finn, this country has elected a fear-mongering, racist xenophobic sexist as its new leader!"

"Whoa Kendra, Kyle said, let's not go that far."

"You know it's true, Kyle, Kendra said, and yet you still choose to support him?"

"I support him because he will restore the moral values of this country. We can't continue down this path of allowing everyone to come here, and I believe he is the one who can help get us back on the right path."

"Seriously, Kyle, you sound just like Baby Frump and his hateful rhetoric. Is this how you intend for people to see you too?"

Finn thought about his brother's words to him today to make a difference and change the world. He thought it was time to try something to at least make a start at it. He knew he was not changing the world, but hopefully, he could get two people not to be so divisive.

"OK, guys, here is the deal. This has been a very shocking election, and it is apparent people have very strong beliefs about it. What we can't do is be torn apart by it. We have to allow it to play out and see if this choice by our country leads to more significant change and, hopefully, not something more drastic."

"While that is true, Finn, Kendra countered, I think Baby Frump is an obnoxious fool that will cause more harm than good. He has no experience, and the only thing he seems to be good at is having companies that file bankruptcy and throwing temper tantrums. This is our new leader?"

"I know Kendra; It is hard to argue the facts. That is why many never expected this to happen, and maybe the country felt that it would not, but it has to play out at this point. Remember the checks and balances that we learned about that are built into our political system? This may be when we see how they work, or it may be possible that he will do a good job, and things will go well."

"Wait, guys, Kyle said. You are both creating so much drama over this. It is what we need, and his talk is just locker room banter. You are both stuck in this bubble of norms where he must act Presidential just to please your tastes. You will see great changes that we are desperate for. That is why he was elected and will be one of our greatest leaders ever."

"You and I have been friends since Kindergarten Kyle, Kendra said. You always told me that you do not see my color and we have shared so many experiences. I just don't see why you do not understand how upsetting this is for me."

"I do get it Kendra, the problem is that your mind is closed to hearing anything you don't want to believe and are not willing to at least see my side as well."

"I cannot continue this conversation, Kyle, Kendra said. You are entitled to your opinion, but I think you are an idiot."

Finn thought about how passionate each of his classmates was about their beliefs in this election. He could tell they were both feeling like most of the country would be feeling. Finn knew that his parents felt Baby Frump was the wrong choice for what they believed in. What he was seeing bothered him, though. What Finn witnessed in his parents, and how he saw Kendra acting was not just about a difference of opinion; it was more of a fear reaction. He wondered, was this something to fear? He decided he would go about his day and just take in what people said and how they were acting.

Throughout the day, Finn saw his classmates who had been friends for years involved in bitter disputes about the outcomes and their hopes. The Frump supporters were ecstatic while the Sillary supporters appeared to be somewhat in shock and somehow angered over this. The Frump supporters cited Sillary's emails, while the Sillary supporters quickly pointed out Frump's stance on immigration and treatment of women.

Other incidents Finn noticed ranged from overall high anxiety among students over increased racial slurs, students mocking Nazi salutes, and derogatory language. This was just day one, what was going to happen as time moves on? He noticed students were targeting each other solely on the candidate they supported. He could not fully grasp how all of these students who had made their way together for years in the same classes were now acting as if they were bitter rivals in a new world. Is it possible one person's words could now cause his friends to behave in the same manner? But then he remembered his feelings and the shock of hearing Baby Frump had won. This was about people not knowing where to place their emotions, as it genuinely was shocking. That was something he felt he needed some answers for. Maybe it would be a good dinner discussion with the family.

When Finn got home from school, he noticed his parents were still unsettled. His Mom told him his Aunt Jean and Uncle Ted were heading into town and would be joining them for dinner. He was excited to see them, as it had been a while since they were all together. He knew his parents would likely feel better once they talked it all out as a family and had a chance to think through the election events. He hoped that with Garrett coming, his insights would bring the calmness they needed.

Finn saw Garrett pulling in, and it did bring Finn a great sense of comfort knowing he was there. He saw Garrett walking up, and he was eyeing up the package he was carrying. Finn was trying to remain calm, but if it was what he hoped, this day was about to get a whole lot better.

Garrett came in and gave Finn a big hug. Finn could not wait.

"So is it possible that package is for me? Finn asked."

"Of course, little brother, and I bet it will make you very happy!"

Finn did not waste a moment tearing into the gift. He could tell it was exactly what he wanted.
"Garrett! It is perfect. It is exactly the laptop I wanted and even in the right color. How did you know?"

"Yeah, right, bro, maybe because you told me exactly what to get!"

Finn's Mom said. "Wow, that looks a bit extravagant for this house. It is a very nice gift."

"Well, Garrett said, school has become so digital now, and Finn will need something that he can transport easily when he goes to college. It will be an excellent resource for his classes."

They all sat in the kitchen while their Mom and Dad were preparing dinner, and Finn was setting up his laptop. Garrett asked their Mom how she was doing, and she admitted that she was still in shock even after having the day to mull it over.

She said, " I believed there was not a chance in hell that fool would win. I guess that is why I have such a hard time adjusting to it."

"You are not alone, Mom, Garrett said. Millions of people are likely feeling the same as you. We have to just move on and trust in the system to control this loose cannon that will be leading the country."

"I know you are right, Garrett, I guess I need time to let it sink in."

Finn thought it would help to interject what he had seen in school as well. "I noticed today that while most of my classmates feel like you, Mom, some of the others are very supportive of giving Baby Frump the opportunity to make changes that may be beneficial. There were indeed many emotions going on, and strong beliefs were on display in abundance."

"I bet you saw a day full of drama, Finn, Garrett said."

"It was a bit intense today, Garrett, that is for sure. Some of the Red party students felt labeled as racist, xenophobic, and lacking character for supporting their parties nominee. Those in the Blue party felt he in no way represented what our country is all about. I think it was clear that we had two candidates that most of the country was not very supportive of backing."

"Well said, Finn, his Dad, told him. I really like how you are examining both points of view to understand working through this."

"I owe it all to Garrett, Finn said. He is the one that talked me through it this morning."

"It's all you little brother, You are the one that wants to make a difference and you are the one setting your course."

"I do have something else about today's events that troubled me. One of the main focuses we learn about in school each year is anti-bullying behavior. What I noticed today appeared to be the opposite of that. I can't figure out how it can just move so quickly to something less desirable. I have seen people arguing about each other's nominee, but now that it is official, it seems to have gotten worse."

"It is because students are molded by what adults say, Garrett said. When your peers hear adults speaking in these terms, it not only directs their thoughts but also gives them the idea that if he can say these things as a leader, I can. The election result basically validated their intent to act as they see fit."

"I can see that part, Finn said. I know what you and Dad and Mom have said over the years has shaped my thinking. I can see now how one person's words can really unleash some damage. I heard some other kids saying how concerning it was that it appears no one is trying to check Frump's words and refute them when they should."

"It is true Dad said, one thing I have learned is not to combat the person but tackle the idea instead. When you challenge the idea, it causes you to focus on the facts and not the individual."

"That is good advice to remember. I think today, I saw the opposite of that with so many heated events unfolding throughout the day. Hey, I see Aunt Jean and Uncle Ted pulling up. Let's get this family love fest started!"

"Happy Birthday, nephew! Uncle Ted said. It is a great day for you and a great day for our nation!"

Oh no, Finn thought, they are Baby Frump supporters? How is it possible two people he had looked up to for years believed in something that did not make sense to him? He was sure his entire family would have the same values and beliefs, but this did not turn out that way. He knew he could handle it but did not feel that his Mom would be very accepting.

"Theodore! His Mom scowled, I thought you were just getting me all lit up when you said you were a Frump supporter? You were really serious about this?"
"Yes sister, he said, It is time for this great change and that time has come today."

"I can't do this, not today, his Mom said. This day is about Finn, not about celebrating the demise of this country."

"Hold on everybody, Garrett said. We can do this and get through it."

"Yes. Dad said, Here is the deal. Ted and Jean are not going to change our minds, and we are not going to change theirs, so it is best to drop it all and end the political discussion so we can move on as a family and enjoy Finn's day. We are all strongly entrenched in our opinions, and arguing with each other is not going to generate some sort of revelation and change our thinking."

"Amen to that, Mom said. Let's move on and end this discussion and enjoy dinner."

"Well, Finn said, I know it is uncomfortable to do this, but if we don't understand each other's views, it is only going to divide us more instead of trying to gain an understanding of why we all feel as we do. Remember what we were just talking about? I think it would be more beneficial to at least express this rather than assuming and labeling each other. This is what I saw happening all day in school, and I do not want this to happen to my family."

"Finn is right, Garrett said. We can't ignore each other, and it is important to understand where each of us is coming from. If we can at least have a civil discussion over dinner and share our views without judgment, it will give us a greater understanding of our choices."

"Well, Dad said, one thing I do know is your Mom, and I raised two incredible boys. Your points are quite valid, and your Mom and I owe it to Ted and Jean just as they need to hear from us what our deciding factors are."

"OK, Mom said, We can talk about it <u>after</u> dinner. I do not want any drama while we are eating. Your Dad and I made a nice dinner, and we will enjoy it as a family."

"Sounds good, Finn said. Let's eat and air it out later."
"Agreed said, Jean, I love that plan. We owe it to each other to understand the motives that lead us to the choices each of us makes."

As dinner went on, Finn thought, did he make a mistake? Was there going to be a battle that was about to happen, and he would end up causing his family to be at odds and unable to bring themselves to remain civil? He thought of what his Dad and Garrett said and knew they could air this out, but emotions sometimes overcome common sense. All Finn could do at this point was hope for the best. He reflected on the morning and thought about how many things had happened since he woke up. What a birthday this was turning out to be, and he was starting to believe this was indeed the turning point, but was it the one he was hoping for?

"Well, Sis, Ted said, you guys have outdone yourselves with this meal. It was incredible."

"I agree, Jean said, you should both open a restaurant! I know Ted wishes I could cook like this."

"Mom and Dad have always had a passion for being in the kitchen and sharing their love of food with others, Finn said. As you can see, my brother and I never go hungry!"

"Speak for yourself, Garrett said. I think I look great!"

"I am just saying maybe we could both stand to lose a few pounds. Uncle Ted, I think since you and Aunt Jean are in the minority at this table, can you share some of the reasons you felt it was the best decision to support Baby Frump?"

"Sure, Ted said, We are looking for someone that can change the country and serve the people instead of the political system. The economy needs something different. While I cringe at some of what he says, at least you know where you stand."

"Jean interjected, I personally could not take any more of Sillary's legacy, and I felt all she would do was lead us directly into war. Baby Frump will bring back much-needed jobs, and he said his cabinet would be filled with the best people. How can you argue with that?"

"Well, you know he is just lying, don't you Jean? Mom said. I am not saying that all politicians tell you what you want to hear, but this man has no experience to do what he thinks he can do. I also think he is dangerous in his thoughts and actions."

"Finn chimed in quickly, no judging here, remember?"

"I can't say we did not discuss our concerns, Sis, Ted said, but we have to trust in a government with its checks and balances in place to control our leader. All in all, we have to decide and vote for what we believe in and what we want to see."

"We can't argue your points, Ted, Dad, said. We just do not see the experience that Sillary has as something we can dismiss, she has the expertise and the know-how, and his crude and obnoxious behavior does not equate to someone that will represent us to the world. Everyone is already laughing at him, and I can't imagine what it is going to look like for our country's image after four years of this made for TV drama."

"She also is the most diverse and will truly represent the entire country. She is fully engaged in criminal justice reform. Black Lives Matter support and many areas that affect all citizens. Mom said."

"When we vote, we have to vote for how it affects us and the changes we want to see, Ted said. We all have our reasons and opinions on what is best. Time is the only thing that can tell us if the choices we made match what we wanted."

Finn was getting a good visual of how two distinct sides had made their choices. Some felt strongly about something to believe in while ignoring the actions and words that spewed from Baby Frump's mouth. His parents wanted something safer and more proven. He could see how these differences could lead to strong opinions and beliefs for each candidate. A person's words and actions show us their real character. He thought of the school posters with a quote, "You Are What You Do, Not What You Say You'll Do." He felt that should be the mantra for all politicians, and he could not help but express that to his Aunt and Uncle.

"You both realize that with this President, our country will go bankrupt, his rhetoric could lead us to a civil war, and no coochie in the country will be safe."

"Finn!! His Mom exclaimed, really?"

"Well, yes, Mom, if you are what you do, this is what he will do."

SIZE MATTERS

Finn had already finished his first semester of college, and it felt good to have that behind him. His family told him it might take time to figure out his path, and he would likely change his mind about his major. He decided to make his decision after his first year as most of his courses were electives, and he had a good idea which way he was headed. He thought a year ago he was so undecided, but as the events of the election unfolded, and the current events seemed so dramatic, he was reasonably confident about which path he would take.

"Garrett! Did you see the briefing on the inauguration?"

"Yes, Finn, the spinning and lying is moving full steam ahead."

"I guess I don't understand how something that is so black and white, with undisputable pictures, can be fabricated into something else."

"Well, Finn, It is because, as we have seen, there are people out there who are willing to buy into it. Some people are just desperate for something to believe in and are eager to go along with untruths and alternative facts to achieve a different outcome. They want to support something they think can make a difference for them. It does not make them bad people; they just view the process and possible outcomes differently. What the Spicy witch is spinning is a spell that will work on so many people because they are also being fed the same untruths on news programs that are directed at getting them to accept it as truth. The good part is that all of the news outlets were quick to refute this because it was obvious. Will there be some people out there that still hold out for it to be true? Absolutely, because that is what drives them. Some want conspiracy theories, and some just need to follow a course that is different than what they have. They are willing to hold on and spread the falsehoods to support their party no matter what reality shows."

"I guess I just find it hard to believe that anyone can rest easy at night knowing they are telling tremendous lies on a platform that reaches millions of people and about something so insignificant such as the size of a crowd."

"Yes, Finn, it is puzzling. But you have to think like someone with the mentality of a child. Baby Frump has an ego that seems to have no end. He cannot stand to be less than anyone else on any terms. So he will dictate to others to spread the stories and spins. This won't be the first. He will bring in many witches to cast the spells of misinformation in hopes of reaching those that want to hear something they can cling to so desperately."

"How will we know what is truth and what is fiction? Our country relies on what our leaders say, and I guess what I am also concerned about is how we would look to the rest of the world when our leader can't be trusted with clear facts. How would he be expected to negotiate with other world leaders, and why would they even take him seriously?"

"Good point, Finn, and a valid concern. One institution that we can rely on heavily is the press and media coverage. There are so many amazing investigative journalists who are out there digging and fact-checking constantly. We can rely on them, however as we have seen, some of them actually will keep spinning the stories even if they are untrue."

"You mean FUXU news?"

"Yes, that is one outlet that you can see caters to Baby Frump's agenda. There are others as well, and that is where we, as a country, owe it to ourselves to listen to both sides and make an educated decision based on the facts. Understanding each other's intentions involves understanding the source of where we receive the information. If we only listen to one news source and that news source has a slanted view that does not represent both sides, then that is all we are going to believe."

"I can see how that makes sense. I know Mom and Dad stick to one news source, and it does shape their thoughts. I guess it would be so hard to figure out what is true and what is a lie unless you can weigh the opposing views and decide. But how do you know?"

"Well, Finn, that requires humans to stop and think, which is something we are not very good at. If we see a shocking headline, we have to ask ourselves, is this something they are trying to get us to buy into? Is it something that is aligned with many biases that exist? If it feeds us information that aligns with what we believe in, then we are more likely to see it as truth. We also have to look at the creator of the article and what sources they are citing to see is it valid and are these people only spreading the same story that seems untrue. Another indicator is looking at the number of media sources with the same story. Each reporter and company will want to have several verified sources. When you see the same story across multiple agencies, it can lend it more credibility as it has a higher likelihood of being vetted."

"That makes sense Garrett, I have heard my friends sharing information that they saw on the news and believe it to be true. They think that just because it was broadcast, it cannot be fake or untrue. It does seem like they are always referring to what they have seen on FUXU news."

"Yes, Finn, the name says it all because that appears to be what it does. These investigative journalists work hard at finding the truth. It is not just about the false statements it is about uncovering things others may be trying to conceal and not want to come to light."

"So true, Garrett. And then we have the "Liar in Chief" saying the media is dishonest. It is so puzzling that he chooses to degrade the office of the presidency his first few days in the role."

"More to come on that for sure. When you already have people filing lawsuits against the President for his business connections and policies in his first week, it cannot turn out well. But there are so many amazing people out there who have chosen the journalism field to ensure the news we receive is true and vetted. It will never stop the people from spreading falsehoods and alternative facts, but knowing that there is always someone checking behind them helps us know when to think twice about what we read and hear. Something else you have to pay attention to is are the different sources just saying broad things with no evidence to back them up? Many times fear will be used based on statements that actually have no truth. When words are said that cause fear and anxiety, many quickly focus on the fear instead of trying to determine if the words are actually valid."

"That is concerning. Fear drives so many things and it can quickly get out of hand and change people's thoughts and actions. His first week international battle about the wall is a good example. Saying another country will build a wall to protect us. Does he think he is the ruler of the world and can dictate what other countries will do? They are more along the lines of "Take your wall and shove it, Frump!"

"Yes! Garrett said, do you think people really believe he was going to have them pay for this? These spins will go well into his tenure, and if he is still around in 4 years, you can bet that the spins will be abundant around the next election. People will really have to dig deep and examine the question, is this true or something they want to believe to be true to secure an election? I guess the question will lie in them asking themselves, "Are his actions really making my life better?"

HER TRUTH IS MARCHING ON

Finn's phone was blowing up with texts from Kendra. He could not keep up with the incoming pics of her at what was being called the "Women's March." Finn texted her to be safe as he could tell there were so many people around her. She replied, " I am here to make sure I am safe, Finn. We have to all do this so that fool understands what he and others say and do to women is not acceptable. We are here to say we are not going away. You can't wish us away, and you can't ignore us. We are what makes this world what it is, and you have had your chance to play your card, and you played wrong!"

Finn thought that over, and he knew she was right. It was essential to address the issue, and he was proud of her for fighting for what she believed in. He was reading this movement was expanding worldwide to combat what many considered anti-women and offensive remarks by Frump. He thought how powerful those words are to be able to spark a worldwide protest. Finn was eager to get back home to talk with his Mom about the day's events. He was shocked, so many people around the world came together to create and participate in this event.

"Hey, Mom!" Have you been following the events of today?"

"You know I have son! It makes my heart feel good to see so many come together for a way to promote social change." This started as one woman proposing an idea, and now it has blossomed to a worldwide event. The crowds are enormous. I bet Baby Frump is boiling over as these crowd sizes have to be double what he had on Inauguration Day!"

"I bet you're right, Finn said. I did not think about that, but it has just to deflate that supersized ego a bit! Maybe you can start a new phrase like "Grab Him By The Ego." or "Large Crowds For The Little Man."

"Finn, you are always so witty. You know your mama is the quiet type and is not going to start a movement of her own. I am content just to watch this take place and support more quietly, like casting my vote for women candidates I believe in."

"Yes, Mom, I think the movement is impressive, and it takes all of us to make a difference somehow. Whether you are marching or casting a vote, it will help promote the change the world wants."
"You know, son, In some ways, what Baby Frump said about women may be a good thing."
"That sounds a little shocking Mom, Tell me more about that."

"Well, as vulgar and offensive as his comments are, it shows that there are some people out there that are willing just to accept it as is. The fact that he was able to get elected even after the comments were made public and played repeatedly shows many in this country appear to be OK with it. The good part is that it motivates people to stand up and pay attention and say wait, this is not OK, and we have to do something better. This will be just the beginning of a more significant movement about how women are treated and what will be a new way of viewing words and actions."

"My friend Kendra was texting me earlier from the march. What you are saying is aligned to why so many out there are acting now to make a difference. Do you think Aunt Jean is having a change of heart over this and now sees her views maybe need to change a bit?"

"I am afraid that is a no son. I called her earlier today and was asking that exact question."

"Wow, I really can't understand how she is still in support of him."

"She said that despite his coarse behavior, she believes he truly understands how women like her are perceived by many in political circles. She thinks that people like Sillary are elitists that frown upon lower-class women. Jean said Frump's policies would promote improvement in the local economy, which is most important to her. She said, "It is more important to her to have an economy that puts food on her table and not getting caught up in his words." She feels like he understands the fight, so many are going through to stay afloat."

"I thought they would see that maybe their choice was not the best, or maybe I was hoping they would have a change of thought. Either way, It is like Uncle Ted said, "You have to vote for the changes you want to see.""

"I also asked her if she would be OK with her daughter dating someone like Baby Frump. She adamantly said, "No. He is vulgar and offensive for sure. I know what his true character is underneath, and he makes me cringe when he speaks, but I can ignore that if he does a good job for the country.""

"I guess I just have trouble understanding that, but I have to appreciate her views and what is giving her the ability to still support someone so demeaning to people.""

"Yes, son, me too. I can see why there are so many strong opinions out there. At first, I did not understand it, but when I gave her the chance to explain, it made me realize that people like Jean are driven by something greater than what others see on the surface. My first thoughts are always to dislike someone I see supporting him, but this is making me realize that I can't dislike or hate them for wanting to believe in something. Their opinions matter even if they are not aligned with my views. I have to say it is a hard thing to do. This is the first time in my life a politician has been able to make me so mad I just want to scream. What makes it worse is that he is a president who should lead the nation and not be circling the toilet with his words and actions. I fear his antics will only get worse and further divide us as citizens."

Finn's phone blew up with another text from Kendra. "OMG Finn, call me."

Finn hoped she had not gotten into trouble somehow. She was too far away for him to get to her quickly. He decided to call her to see what she needed.

"Kendra!" Are you OK?"

"Finn, no, not really. I mean I am safe here, but my cousin just called and saw me on TV at the March."

"Was she excited?"

"No, she was so mad to see me at this march and told me I had no business here and to let Baby Frump do his job!"

"What? So even with all of his racially charged comments, you have family members that support him?"

"Yeah, she said many people her age feel the other party has taken us for granted for so long and have done nothing to promote the changes needed. She said while we have primarily leaned toward this party time after time, things never change, and she was electing someone that could stir it up and create that change. I really can't wrap my head around it, Finn. I just see her party as old white men that cite the holier than thou values but live their lives entirely differently. They are quick to proclaim their Christian beliefs but behind closed doors the story is so different and shameful for them just like what Baby Frump does. They use one hand to hold up a bible and the other to fondle men and women below the belt!"

"It is shocking for sure, Kendra. I am glad you were able to talk it out with her and at least see her side of it."

"Well, I listened, but you know my temper and my convictions Finn, Once she got done scolding me, I told her she was born into the wrong family and hung up on her."

"Ouch, Finn said. Kendra, I know how heated all of this is, and these times are not going to get better with constant fighting. I was shocked by my family as well, but once we talked over some of our underlying motives, it helped make it less about us versus them and more about what we can all do together. I know how passionate you are, Kendra, and I do not blame you for being shocked and reacting. I wish you would call her and try to make amends and find some common ground to move forward. Your family is too important, and so is what is at stake here."

"Why do you always have to be so damn extra Finn? You are like a life coach on steroids!"

"I will send you a bill, just call her and work it out. I can see how some of your family likes his actions on criminal justice and reforms that align with them. I guess I just can't get past his comments that are so racially charged they are impossible to ignore."

"Me too, Kendra said. I guess when Frumpie asked "What have you got to lose?" maybe they will realize exactly what that was as time goes on."

"Yes, Finn said. Time will tell for sure. Now be safe and work this out with your cousin."

"OK, I promise to sleep on it and figure it out tomorrow."

"Good, now be careful and let me know how it goes."

Finn thought about his conversation with his Mom and Kendra over the next few weeks, and wanting a way for people to see each other's viewpoints without being so divisive. How could he be a voice for people to be less combative, let their walls down, and instead of trying to change each other's minds, let each other speak and explain? He saw so many arguments between opposing sides. If only he had that power, he felt he could make such a difference. But how can one teenager be the voice for a country of divided people?

UNPRECEDENTED

Finn was excited today as he was meeting Garrett for lunch. It felt like forever since they were able to get together and talk. He always enjoyed their conversations and his brother's thoughts on the events.

"Hey, Garrett, thank goodness we can get together and have some sanity."

"Why Finn, what's going on?"

"Mom and Dad are just furious."

"What did you do, Finn?"

"I am the good son, remember, it's not me. Well, at least, not this time."

"Wait, How can we both be the good son?"

"Well, since you were born way before me, you had more years of being the good son, so now it is my turn."

"OK, I will give you that. What is all the drama about?"

"Mom and Dad are just furious and consumed over this whole immigration policy issue and how Baby Frump just goes and fires the Attorney General just because she does not agree with his insanity."

"Well, it does look like that, and I am sure he was just looking for every opportunity to get rid of her as she had warned him about many things he disagreed with. However, what he did was perfectly legal and according to the constitutional powers. While I applaud her stand, and as insane as his immigration policies are, it just became a procedural issue. I find it ironic that this is a man that follows no established norms and procedures, yet when it is in his favor, it allows him to do what he wants."

"So, she was doing a good thing for the country's values, yet the way it happened just turned out to be a procedural issue?"
"Yes, many people would rather not take a stand like she did and risk losing their position. She likely knew what would happen, but it did not stop her from fighting for a more significant outcome. Once again, we see a new movement form as a result of the immigration issues."

"But isn't Frump married to an immigrant? How is it he hates immigrants, yet he lives with one?"

"So he is operating under the guise of illegal immigrants. This has been his focus and his attempts at instituting his travel ban, which thankfully was blocked. I am still not sure if that is his focus or if he is racist against the majority of immigrants, legal or illegal. Remember when you talked about that quote, "You are what you do, not what you say you'll do," He says a lot of things that appear extremely racist like his comments about Mexicans being rapists and drug dealers. When people tend to make sweeping statements about a particular class of people or country, you know where their true intentions lie. It was not as if he had singled out an individual or specific group of Mexicans; he labeled them all."

"Yes, and I saw he has more than just these incidents. It appears he has been making racists comments for many years. Speaking of his words, did you ever notice he always says, "Believe Me" or "In a very short period of time"?

"I know, right! It is like when people say, "I am not lying," you know they are! He uses that to try and add to his lack of credibility. Anytime someone has to say "Believe Me" you know they are about to lie or at least hope you are going to agree with what they say." when he says "In a very short period of time" he is giving people something to hold onto that they are longing for when the reality is nothing ever happens. He has already promised news conferences and meetings and new orders that never materialize when he says that, but people hold out hope that it will happen."

"So, he just seems full of bluster and lies and throws anything out there that may stick. He is very good at branding. All of his hype is nothing more than a marketing scheme that people fall for?"

"Yes, as with all politicians, there is always a certain amount of bluster. The difference is he consistently tells bald-faced lies with it instead of just being honest. Our citizens need honesty to make the right choices not false truths and conspiracies that have no validity."
"Is that why he called the press "The Enemy of the American People"?

"He is trying to blame them for his ineptitude. Instead of being responsible, he is lashing out at news organizations for catching him in his web of lies and deceit. His language and words are very dangerous and come with great meaning as he speaks from a significant office. It is up to the free press to point this out and make sure we as citizens are informed and can see through the charade."

"Yet, it still comes back to his supporters that agree with him and now hate the press?"

"Unfortunately, they will back whatever he says even if it is a lie. And the worst part is we have media groups that continue these lies and conspiracy theories to enhance the divide further."

"So, FUXU News is just there to support him?"

"No. they are supposed to be journalists and report impartially. However, they are clinging to the drama to make some money and put a spin on it all to go along with whatever Frump says. One day, Baby Frump will be gone, and they will be left to answer for their charades."

"I just saw something like this being reported. There's some fool of a representative Devil Oozeness that tried to support the wiretapping mockery they were trying to create. He was running around like a weasel in the night, offering false proof these conspiracies were true."

"Yes, and he even held a press conference to further dig a hole he will be unable to recover from."

"I guess what I don't understand is that if these are elected officials supposed to be for the people and uphold the checks and balances of the system, why are they supporting lies and conspiracy theories and creating more lies to go with them?"

"Well a lot of it has to do with blaming the previous administration and trying to find fault to make themselves look good or heroes of the people. The reality is that they are in control of their choices and will have to live with the consequences. That is what bothers me, how do they face their family and have their legacy written as co-conspirators of these government disasters?"

"I know what Dad has always told us, "When you lay your head on your pillow at night, rest easy knowing you have lived your day honestly and did the best you could. When your conscience is clear, you can rest easy and proud."

"He always said that! It took me a while to figure it all out, but it is so true. When you do things as you should, there is nothing you have to cover-up for or worry about."

"You know, Garrett, Dad was saying how concerned he was about how Baby Frump is putting all of these people in cabinet positions with no experience for these roles. He said he is taking his cronies and building a swamp like no one has ever seen."

"He has good reason to be concerned. Placing people in these influential roles with no experience is indeed a way to end in disaster. I think it is only a matter of time that the turnover in many positions will be intense as no one will want to work under the made for TV disaster. What is even worse is how he is doing it to his family as well. These people have zero experience, and yet they qualify as trusted advisors? It is also challenging to figure out the truth and reality these days. Remember how we talked about the Spicy witch casting spells of disinformation across the country? It appears that it just keeps going. Did you see the voter fraud conspiracy tweets?"

"I did Garrett, It all seems confusing because they are citing research evidence, so how does a person know how legitimate it is?"

"So true, Finn, however, the research cited was from 5 years ago, completely unrelated to this election, and the study was found to be erroneous and debunked by members of its own survey team."

"I guess you really have to pay attention to know fact from fiction. It seems what they are relying on is just accept what we say and believe we would not lie to you and expect people to fall for it."

"Yes, you do, and now more than ever, as we have already seen, this administration will leave no lie on the table if it makes them appear legitimate."

"OK, Bro, as always, I love having these conversations. Let's make sure we stay consistent in getting together. I think if the past few months are any indication, we will have plenty to talk about. I still remember your guidance about how to really look at articles, and the validity of them, thanks to some skilled journalists doing the job they do."

"You know it, Finn."

Finn knew that was true. Each day brought with it some new story. It amazed him how many times he heard that the actions of Baby Frump were unprecedented. He was making changes, but were they for the better? Were these changes that even his supporters wanted to see? Finn thought this couldn't be happening. He woke up to see a news story that Frump compared the size of his nuclear button to Kem Youngone. He thought it just never stops with him. Why is he still allowed to have a phone and an account to blast whatever is on his mind? He already knew, though, that was the issue. No one could control him or even willing to try. His people were constantly on clean up detail, making spins on his statements and making it appear that he was saying was not how it was perceived. Finn also noticed 34% of his high-level staff had turned over in the first year. He wondered is our country that numb?

Over the next few days, he saw that Frump had dissolved the commission on voter fraud after finding no evidence of voter fraud. Would his followers recognize that this conspiracy was over, or were they still going to hang in there? Would it resurface again in a few years so Baby Frump can blame something else for his failures? He saw a white supremacist group cheering on his policies and saying how well they aligned to their ideals. They even praised his State of the Union address. He thought that was very telling. If white supremacists love you and your ideals, I guess that should be pretty apparent what your views are.

SPINNING WITCHES GO ROUND AND ROUND

Finn thought about how much happened since he graduated from high school. He could not believe he was already in his 2nd year of college and the path he was creating for himself. His career choice was a perfect fit for him. It would give him the ability to make the difference he wanted in a way he could be expressive and most importantly, honest. He thought of all of the witches as he and his brother called them spinning stories from the Baby Frump press office. He thought of the original Spicy Witch and the beginning of what he called the Frumpy Fallacies that had started it all and what it has led to from that podium. The fact that the crowd size was so easily refutable and backed up with made-up photographs and additional lies baffled him to this day. It was definitely the first incantation of many more to come. It set the tone for what amounted to over 7,000 falsities so far, so many were still in support of these spins on reality.

Finn was stunned by someone's ability to create so many false narratives and spin the truth so far out of control that it leaves the country confused, dazed, and not sure what can be believed any longer. He wondered what the point behind so many tales was, as the truth is always seen, so why create the spins that would be disproven? Finn also realized that no one was really stopping these lies. While there were many out there able to fact check, many others allowed this behavior to continue to deceive unchecked and without boundaries. Why would a leader choose to wear down the citizen's so bad that they become numb? In the end, he could only think of one thing...winning. The childish little Frump had to win at everything, no matter how much it hurt the country's citizens. At any cost, he had to win; at any cost, he had to be the decision-maker, at any cost, he could not ever look bad. Finn knew it was also more than just winning. Could it be for monetary gain as well? He felt this may end up being the most corrupt President ever to reside in that office. There had to be truth behind so many stories out there, and if they were not true, why would Frump spend so much time evading them and creating so many falsities and rebuttals. Many have paid the price for his actions and stood at that podium and spun the truth to support him and create a cover for his lack of common sense.

The tales Spicy told were so easily refuted. Yet, it did not stop him from claiming that Frump had the most electoral votes and that there were millions of fraudulent votes and fictitious wiretapping concerns. All of this because the little Frump could not ever look bad. He thought of the Huckleberry witch and her web of deceit that ensued. What makes it worse is both of them admitted to lying to our country at a time when they should have been defending our values and not engaged in a mockery of the political system. The Homey saga was a big deal. Many lies were spun about the events that it became an entangled mess until it was brought to light that both witches had just been covering for a leader who built his legacy on lies. They both ran public cover for the circumstances around asking Homey for his loyalty, who decided to fire Homey, and what Baby Frump asked Homey to do. What Finn found remarkable was not that they ran the cover-up, but that they did it from a place of extreme importance that many relied on actually to be the truth. Standing in front of millions of people and lying about something that damages the entire nation was so unacceptable to Finn. He remembered there was another short-lived witch as well. He could barely recall his name but thought it was something like Antoonie Lotsasmoochie. He was a character who seemed to want to erase his past; however, one can never run from themselves. Finn thought, he does deserve credit for trying to make amends though.

He knew the parties were getting more and more divided, but to him, it was not a matter of the parties being against each other it was about how the entire country should be against its adversaries. How would people rather stand up for a liar than defend a nation so great? How did it get to the point of looking away from the facts to support what Finn considered criminal acts? The Huckleberry witch just kept spinning tales of agents losing faith in Homey, The AG's involvement, and the dictation of memos by a president to cover up acts of shame and disgrace to a country. Frump admitted to his hush-money payments, and yet she said he did not. She falsely claimed he never promoted or encouraged violence when he did. He even promised to pay legal fees to those who he asked to incite violent acts. The final straw for Finn was when Frumpy encouraged police brutality, and she claimed he was joking. What made it more remarkable to Finn was the number of people that continue to cover for him, including so many members of his inner circle and even his family. He knew that he and Garrett would have a great conversation when they had time to sit and talk.

WHY

Finn was thinking about how time had passed so quickly. He was eager to start his adult life and college. It seemed like it took forever for him to reach eighteen, but now he felt like his life was moving at warp speed. His college years were almost behind him. He did feel wiser, but still had so many lingering questions, or maybe they were actually concerns. He felt relieved, though, as he knew today would help ease those concerns as he waited for Garrett. As always, he felt better when they could talk things out and share views. He saw Garrett waiting for him, and it just gave him a sense of calm and happiness.

"There he is! Finn, the world's greatest journalist!"

"Hey, Garrett! One day maybe, but not yet. I have so much learning left to do and so many unanswered questions."

"Well, you will always have unanswered questions, Finn, and your studies are so close to being complete. You have made such a great choice for yourself. Remember how you have always been so intent on making a difference? This is how you will do it."

"Yes, I can't wait to see what I can do, but why do I feel so uneasy about it?"

"It is normal to have concerns about significant changes and something new, Finn. When you face those fears is how you will grow. You know that I have made so many changes throughout my life, some I was not sure I should do. But, what I do know is as uneasy as I was during that time when I had a chance to reflect on it, I saw how much I was able to grow personally and professionally. Those changes exposed me to so many things that I would likely never have experienced. What you are feeling is healthy and exciting." Life is an adventure, so enjoy it no matter what path it takes you on."

"Yes, I can see how it has helped you be so wise to the world."

"But you know what Finn, I still learn new things every day."

"I guess I am just afraid of saying or doing the wrong thing."

"Even the most celebrated journalists in the world will make mistakes, Finn. It is part of the business that sometimes information is only as good as the sources you have; mistakes will be made. You just own up to it and move on. I feel like your concerns may be around the statements from the Frumpy Fallacy Foray."

"Nice alliteration, bro."

"I was saving it to impress you!"

"Yes, I guess it is really bothering me. Why would he call the press the enemy of the people when all they are doing is a legitimate job?" It just seems so disrespectful to such an established industry."

"Well, he acts like he is running an autocratic regime for one. He lives in a fantasy world, believing that anyone that does not agree with him can be admonished. He can't stand the fact that people are free to their opinions, and when they point out his lies and fallacies, he can only start spreading fake news in an effort that someone will actually believe him."

"Mom is concerned with all of the threats against journalists that I may be entering the wrong profession."

"You know Mom; she is just expressing her concerns for her baby, She knows that you have to do this and you will be amazing. The world is smart and can see through a fool. People are free to make up their minds, and even if some will buy into his lies, after time, they will see the light when he is long gone and forgotten."

"Yes, I guess it is because Mom and Dad have been so upset about so many things lately. It takes a toll on me and shapes my thoughts when I should be making my own decisions. Do you remember when we played the "Why" game when I was little?"
"Of course! You were the world's most curious child, I think." It was always why, why, why, no wonder you are entering the world of investigative journalism."

"I guess so; I feel like we need to do an adult version of this."

"Let's do it. What's on your mind?"
"Well, a lot. I just think I need to talk it out with you. I have the influences from home and school, and I know I need to make up my mind. I guess I am looking for some sage advice from someone impartial that has more life experience at this."

"Ouch, that makes me feel old."

"You know what I mean."

"I do, but it makes me think about my younger years when I was looking for the same thing."

"You already helped me through my first question!"

"You have more?"

"Well, I may or may not have made a list."

"Fire away, brother, fire away."

"Well, my why's are plentiful. Why would a leader call his top justice department and FBI officials the "Deep State" it seems like that goes against why those departments exist. I can only imagine it is to spin some conspiracy theory, but he was elected, so what is he telling lies like that for?"

"Exactly the point, Finn. Conspiracy theories so people will take pity on the poor Baby Frump, and he would hope to gain more support when people could view him as a victim. You will notice a theme when you look deeper. These lies he spews are all done to distract people from the real issues he is up against. When his back is to the wall, he will create a new spin or conspiracy to take the attention away from what makes him look bad."

"OK, that ties many things together for me. When Frump said his former campaign CEO, Cannon, had lost his mind was just a cover because he really had dirt to spill?"

"You got it."

"I thought it was hilarious when he tried to stop the White House expose from being published by having his lawyer send a cease and desist, and they actually published it earlier instead!"

"Yes, you gotta love how karma plays itself out sometimes. What makes me laugh is this is a man that people ridicule every time he opens his mouth, yet he dares to label himself a "very stable genius," hoping to create a new brand for himself."

"It is all about branding with him, isn't it?"

"Yes, Finn, it is what he built everything on, well almost everything that didn't already fail or show it's illegality."

"I was thinking it is all about repeating those words and phrases he always uses which are lies, but he turns them into a brand as he figures the more people hear them over and over there is a likelihood they will be believable."

"You mean phrases like," many people are saying," "in a very short period of time," "there are going to be big changes coming up," and nothing ever materializes?"

"Yes, brother, those, and so many more! My other why is how can he be obstructing justice by calling for the special counsel to be dismissed?"

"He will try anything, but thank goodness there are those who have the sanity to stop him. He has no boundaries."

"I know Garrett, what baffles me if he has nothing to hide why does he spend so much time creating all of these ways for the truth to not come out?"

"Where there's smoke, there's fire brother, where there's smoke there's fire."

"So true, I saw report he would even tear up documents that would have to be taped back together so there would not be a violation of the Presidential Records Act. I read an article that said a letter was ripped into tiny pieces from Shuck Fumer." Talk about someone being passive-aggressive!"

"It is like he lives in a parallel universe where nothing exists unless it is in his mind!"

"Mom was furious over the whole immigration statement. When I got home one day, she was so mad, saying, "Guess what Frumpty Dumpty said! He actually said he hated the children being taken away, and he hated having parents and children separated." She was so mad Garrett because it was his "Zero Tolerance" policy that was causing it!"

"On man Finn, I can hear her ranting and raving now!"

"Why would someone always make themselves look bad by constantly saying stupid things, Garrett?"

"Give me an example."

"I can probably give you thousands, but he also said there was a report that exonerated him from collusion when the actual report was about the Sillary emails and had nothing to do with the special counsel investigation."

"Yes, I remember that one. I don't have a good answer other than what else would one expect. When a person is desperate for believers, they will pull out all of the stops."

"Why would he put so many in his cabinet that were so corrupt? He ran to drain the swamp and filled it with many no-experience cronies that resigned over all of their unethical behaviors. Look at Snott Doodit. He had to resign amidst investigations from fifteen federal agencies. There is Tommy the PriceisRight spending our money to fly charter jets everywhere, Dave Showmeyourmoney accepting lavish gifts, Ry Stinky, who will spare no taxpayer expense to get home. Den, the Decorator, thought the HUD office means bringing the whole family along for the free ride. Comrade Will, who was a bit to close to the puppet master Vlady."

"Stop Finn, you are cracking me up, and I will pee my pants from laughing! But, I know what you mean, so many ethical issues all over the place and he can't keep a body in place anywhere! Speaking of the puppet master, why do you think Frump is always on his side?"

"I know he actually defends him over our own national intelligence. And he said he saw no reason why it would be Vlady interfering in our election, and then tried to backtrack it a bit too late. From what I have gathered, Frump has an affinity for him and his leadership, and he probably could not have won the election without Vlady's interference. I think Sillary was spot on when she called him his puppet."

"I have to agree with that. Only he knows the exact answer, but his actions certainly back up your theories. Just so damn puzzling why he puts his adversaries interest over those of his own citizens. Not only this but defending a country and pledging loyalty to them after they dismembered a journalist. Maybe it has something to do with the 500 rooms they booked at his hotel."

"Once the investigation is over, it will all come to light and be handled."

"Do you think it will be the bitter end of the Frumpian legacy?"

"I don't know, as long as his party leaders keep looking the other way for him, it may not. There is some light ahead, though, as I saw several members were attempting to file an impeachment resolution against the Deputy AG, but other members of the Frump party asked for it to be stopped, and it was. So sometimes people do have the courage to do the right thing!"

"Our country is doing the right thing by replacing so many seats in the last midterm elections with more diverse and legitimate candidates. I consider it a slap in the face to Frump and his allies that enough is enough of his tyrannical tendencies."

"You gotta love his ringmaster in this circus, Tootie Doodioni who says no collusion, then says well if there was, is it really a crime? What's the real story here, Tootie? You get in trouble as much as Frump every time you speak! Oh, and your "Truth isn't Truth" quote is absolutely priceless! And the icing on the cake is the First lady has a campaign against cyber bullying and who is the biggest cyber bully in the world…Frumpo!"

"You are really getting the whole story, Finn! Your education is paying off, and you are on such a great track right now. This is a perfect time for you to see how a true journalist can take pride in what they do and why there is such a need for the truth."

"Thanks, Garrett. I think I just need the reinforcement to keep going. I can tell this is what I feel like I should be doing, especially now, to stand up for what is right. I was so happy to see many press corps come together to defend this industry's integrity."

"It is incredible Finn, that in this time of our lives we have to do that. So many of the founding principles are being put to the test anymore. I think all of what we have gone over shows something fundamental. Baby Frump has gotten into something that is above his pay grade. While he is driven by power, he has no experience or expertise in such a role. In many ways, all of this is just something he should never have stepped into."

"I can see your point, Garrett. All of these issues could have arisen from a lack of knowledge. I guess it would be wiser to listen to your advisors instead of fighting them."

SEE THE EVIL BUT SPEAK NO EVIL

"Hey, Mom! What's the good word?"

"Well, Finn, it seems harder and harder these days to find good words. "What I know is good is you are in your final year of college, and you will do such wonderful things. So proud of you for your commitment and passion for making a difference."

"Thanks, Mom. I have an essay to write that has been weighing on me that I need to get right. I want to put my heart into it and make it meaningful."

"I can help you, son."

"Thanks, I know you would, but I have to do it myself from my own perspective. If I am going to be an amazing journalist that I want to be, then I have to express my own opinions and convictions."

"Yes, you do, and yes, you will, son! It seems like my days have all been consumed by these impeachment hearings. I can't seem to walk away from it. It is important, and I want the best information possible, but the drama between the parties is intense. I did not think three years ago Baby Frump would last this long, but here we are still going at it, and it appears that the country remains even more divided."

"I know. Some of my friends say they just have to walk away from the news as it is nonstop and become frustrated or depressed by it. It is important, but I can see how it can be overwhelming."

"They are announcing the vote results now. I am afraid I already know from his parties' comments about where they stand how this will unfold."

"Well, there you go, Mom, the vote is to acquit. Does this mean he is off the hook?"

"Your Dad was saying even with the acquittal vote; he is still impeached. He will just stay in office, spinning more lies and ruining our country's image until he can be replaced. As horrible as this has been, son, I am glad you can participate in it. It just gives additional credence to where you are going with your life and how important it is to make sure all evidence is clear and forthcoming."

"I know, Mom, if this had not all played out, I wonder if many would truly understand just how important all of this is."

"I am having a family dinner this weekend, Garrett, and your Aunt and Uncle are coming. It will be great to see the different viewpoints after all of this has played out."

"That will be good. Hopefully, we can all act in a sane and civilized manner. At school, the arguments and fighting are very intense. So many are unable to even have rationale conversations without yelling and name-calling. It is as if once someone finds out your political leanings, you are immediately labeled and grouped into a set that may or may not match your true intentions."

"Son, that is so true, and I have to remind myself of it when I run across it in my interactions. Something that really helped me was the other day, Dad and I watched Lil' Maherganja. He said something that resonated with me profoundly. He said something like you could hate Frump; you can't hate the people who like him. I thought well, that is true. My first instinct is always to be disgusted when I find out someone I know or love supports this man, but it is not as if they are making his decisions and words. They want something different and have a right to seek it out."

"OK, that is very powerful, Mom. I will remember it, and I think you just helped unknowingly with my essay."

"That's what Mom's do, Finn. We are there even when you do not know you need us!"

Finn thought about that conversation a lot in the next few days. He knew those words were significant in what was playing out across the country. He heard people being divided with no middle ground to come together. He heard Frump spewing bitter, divisive language. He knew there had to be a way people could find their commonalities and move on together instead of apart. Tonight's dinner would likely give him new insights as well. He was looking forward to family time, even if it was uncomfortable for him.

As he and Garrett were setting the table for dinner, they remembered the last time they had a family event was to celebrate Finn's 18th birthday and the drama that unfolded that evening. It seems like such a long time ago now, but they were both eager to see if their Aunt and Uncle's perspectives had changed.

"Garrett, do you think they paid attention to all of this and just ignored it?"

"We shall see, Finn. It is important for sure. We have to see where they are now and if it makes sense from their viewpoint."

"That is true. It is very challenging to be calm when you feel so passionate about something. What started out as another election that I really never paid much attention to has now seemed to consume everyone's life."

"It really has Finn. But in an essential way, if you are not paying attention, and do not participate, this is what you end up with."

"There are Aunt Jean and Uncle Ted now!"

"Finn! How has your college experience been?"

"Well, Uncle Ted, In some ways, what I thought and in others, nothing like I have ever experienced. I have learned so much, though, and have grown from it for sure. I feel more independent and in charge than I did in high school."

"That is awesome. We are very proud of you and can't wait to see what you will do with your career."

"I have to say, I was a bit hesitant about how you would react when you found out. I mean, your President is not too fond of those in my profession as it stands now."

"Well, Finn, just because your Aunt and I voted for him does not mean we agree with everything he does. We think your choice is perfect and it is needed. As we have seen, many things that have been uncovered would have gone undocumented if it had not been for good journalists."

"That is right, Finn, his Aunt, said. You have to do this, so we count on someone out there who is willing to uncover the truth."

"Let's talk about it while we eat. I know your Mom is not pleased if her meals are cold when she serves them, and I am not about to make my sister mad."

"That is right, brother! Now let's all sit down and enjoy this meal and each other's company."

Finn had just seen how easy it was for people to make assumptions and convince themselves what others would think. He was worried his Aunt and Uncle would be disappointed because of all of the "fake news" language circulating from their spewer in chief. He was concerned they would act like so many others he had witnessed that just bought into the whole conspiracy. If they could see the facts, why were so many others unable to he thought?

"Mom, this meal is so delicious. We have had this before, but it just tastes extra special to me for some reason."

"I know why Finn, Uncle Ted, said. You have been eating so much of that cafeteria prepared food at school, and you forgot what real food tastes like."

"I guess so, but damn, I may not stop. While I am stuffing my face, can you tell us if you still feel the same now about Baby Frump compared to when he was elected."

"Remember when your Aunt and I voted for him, we wanted changes. He did bring us some of those things we were looking for. Some of those included his reshaping of the federal judiciary with new Supreme Court justices and other judges."

"Oh, you mean the high moral character ones they managed to push through brother? Mom said."

"Just because they are conservative judges does not mean they will do everything Frump does. While they may lean to a particular party, they are still judges to uphold the law. Another big thing for us was the tax cuts he was able to accomplish."

"You mean the tax cuts for his crooked corporate friends, Dad said."

"I can't argue that there are many benefits for corporations, Ted said. But, what I hope for is that with the increased benefits to corporations, it leads to higher wages for employees and a boost for the economy."

"Well, you have more faith in that than me, brother. Mom said"

"We will see Sis, but you have to agree his First Step Act on reforming the criminal justice system is huge."

"That I do brother, it was much needed, but I believe anyone could have accomplished it as it had bipartisan support for so long."

"But they didn't get it done, he did."

"OK, brother, well played...well played."

Everyone had a good chuckle over that. Finn was thinking even after everything Baby Frump had done since his election, his Aunt and Uncle still believed in him and supported him on specific issues that affected them. What struck him as significant tonight was two opposing sides finding their commonalities.

"You know what made my heart feel good was when he was able to take out one of the world's most wanted terrorists. Jean said."

"Cheers to that, Mom and Dad said simultaneously."

"Good points, Ted, Mom said. But do you just look the other way when there are so many things he does that are just unacceptable?"

"It would be impossible to look the other way, Sis. This is where Jean and I are let's say more than disappointed and often outraged over his words and behaviors. Remember when we said we had concerns over his actions when we chose him as our candidate, we had hoped it would just be the hype about getting elected, and that he would turn it around once in office. Well, we were very wrong about that for sure."

"Yes, Jean said, Ted and I agree that he should have done a completely different job of bringing people together instead of choosing to divide a nation. His comments around the neo-nazi rally's events were not only astounding to us; they were obviously meant to stir the pot intentionally. The other big thing for me is the total separation of children and families. He imposed this and then tried to blame the previous administration for it. The whole policy is shameful."

"Oh, Jean! I am so glad you feel that way, Mom said. I am distraught over those actions as well, and it is good to know that even someone who supports him can still see the balance that needs to exist in all of this."

"Well, it amounts to basic decency for all human life. Did you think Ted and I would believe anything different?"

"No, Jean, I guess it has been hard for me not to create these assumed labels about how the different sides feel just because they support him. I should know better that you and Ted would see what is right. We should have been staying in touch more instead of avoiding discussions so we could see where our similarities and differences are instead of assuming."

Garrett and Dad chimed in at the same time with a "Well Said." Finn could feel the tensions lift and see how relaxed the family was becoming. He made a note of how just a small bit of communication can change perceptions and assumptions. He wanted to know so much more about their different thoughts on so many things. He saw that this discussion was not about changing each other's minds but just understanding what was on them. He knew that was why it was not some escalated quarrel.

"Finn asked. So what else do you think could have been handled better or done differently?"

"Ted responded, You know how he thinks he is the only one that can make a decision?"
"Yes, dad said. His "I alone can fix it comments" will go down in history and not in a good way."

"It appears that he also believes that is how it should go for our country by pushing away all of our allies that we have created bonds with for so long and have much history with." His ability to embarrass not only himself but also the country on the world stage is intensely infuriating to me. No matter how much cover-up his aides try to do, he is just relentless about it. It is as if it is always my way or no way at all with him,"

"I am with you on that, Uncle, Garrett said. For me, it is also how he just decides to pull out of the Climate Accord without heeding any of the long-term impacts and benefits."
"Yes, we agree; it is not about mistreating a country; it is about treating the world properly and taking care to do the right things to protect the planet. The good news is many states have started initiatives to combat this, so it is not lost, and we can rejoin."

"How do you feel about his actions on what he has done in the Middle East?"

"I have to rate those as failures, Garrett. It is a clear abandonment of the allies we have worked so hard to create."

"Finn said, I think this all goes back to what you and I talked about Garrett. He is just out of his area of expertise in this role as President."

"I have to agree with a lot of that, Ted, Said. It definitely shows through in many of his actions."

"It sounds like you guys have had a change of heart over your political leanings? Are you changing sides? Mom asked."

"No, we still like the core values of our party, we just may disagree with how the leader of it, and other party members choose to conduct themselves. Jean and I believe this impeachment process was very challenging to watch and buy in to. It does not take as a scholar to see what Baby Frump did. It should have been enough to remove him from office, but in a divisive world, it appears our party chose to be on the side of politics instead of what was best for the country as a whole."

"That is what confuses me, Finn said. If it was so clear that what Frump did was obstruction and against the norms of this country and its foundation of impeaching for high crimes and misdemeanors, why did the overwhelming majority of his party not see this as the right thing to do for the country?"

"Well, they did, Finn, Dad said. But they chose a different path based on public perceptions and the perceived need to unite behind their party."

"That is correct, Uncle Ted said. It is not as if the party did not precisely know what they were doing by choosing to play a game of willful blindness instead of admitting that Frump's actions were wrong. My frustration is that they chose to normalize the unacceptable behavior and set a new precedent for future presidents to behave in the same manner. They had an opportunity to set a new course to keep our country strong but instead set us on a course that shows presidential corruption is OK. In the words of your man, Adam the Orator, "You may think that's OK. But I don't think it's OK."

"Mom burst out, That speech had me in tears, and I thought it would change the trajectory of how events would play out. But it seemed to make no difference at all. Why do you think your party chose to look the other way even with compelling evidence and admissions by Slick Noshamey that Frump did hold up the funds?"

"All in the name of politics and public perception, Sis. If the Frump party had the guts to admit what he did was wrong, the public would have been more agile in their thinking. Instead, they chose to make it yet another divisive battle. With the public expressing only a 49% disapproval, they knew it would need to be as high as 60% to remove him without causing disruption. but because they saw the evil he did and chose to say nothing about it, public perception led politicians to keep their mouths shut and follow party lines." Flimsy Grohm and Snitch McBobble both said they would not even be impartial, sending the message that their minds were made up and so should the rest of the country's before even witnessing the trial."

"Jean interjected. "What I have a hard time wrapping my head around was how this entire party could lay their heads on their pillows at night, and sleep soundly, knowing what they were doing was causing the country to further decline instead of standing up for what makes it great."

"I agree with that comment, Jean, Mom, said. I have been struggling with putting all of this together in my head. I am glad we can share these ideas and try and develop our understanding of the events."

"Finn said, I can't imagine having to explain the rest of my life how my father or mother chose to take the side of a divisive leader instead of doing what is right for the country. These people are supposed to represent us, and instead, they decide to put their party ahead of their own citizens. What a legacy to leave for your family to have to answer to for years to come."

"Luckily for you, Finn, Mom said, you have a family that knows how to make rational decisions."

Finn was amazed at how the conversation just flowed and brought everyone together. Even though the differences remained and the family still chose separate political parties. The common issues brought what was essential to focus on. You can't have one side protecting the country while the other side is walking a thin line between what is right and criminality. Finn thought, what do we do now? How can we see these differences and come to the common ground when the division in the country is so intense? Wait, he already knew the answer they had talked about on his 18th birthday.

"Well, Finn said, I guess we vote!

"I could see your mind going, Finn, Garrett said. Tell us more!"

"When you do not like what is going on, you vote to make the change. That is why we have elections. It is obvious the current members of the party have shown their true colors. We can no longer rely on them to do what is right but instead, what is convenient for their careers and their party. Remember, when the students at the high school where the shootings happened said to our leaders, "Make some changes, or we will vote you out!" That is precisely what we have to do."

"Exactly, Dad said, that is just what the system is set up to do. Make changes when a change needs to happen."

"What do you think you will do in the next election, Uncle Ted?"

"You know Garrett; it is evident that Baby Frump is just too dangerous for another four years. We gave him the chance to set us on a new course, and while he did a few things we liked, he has overwhelmingly changed this country in a way we can no longer accept. The racial divide, catering to foreign adversaries, and the man's ineptitude make it clear our vote will not be cast for him. Your Aunt and I see nothing wrong with voting outside of our party when so much is at stake. We need a real leader to be able to bring this country back to its founding values. Maybe we do not agree with all of Jojo's values and plans, but he can be a leader and bridge the divide that is getting deeper by the day. I never thought I would witness a president making comments that are so out of touch with reality. We have seen we are unable to rely on the checks and balances that have catered to him instead of the constitution. Our citizens are worth more than one party's mission for disaster. If we do not make a change now we may be unable to recover."

"So true, Mom said. He has shown his words are his truth and cannot be denied even though he makes every effort to. It just infuriates me when his little soldiers cover for him and his words saying he was joking, or that is not what he meant. They think that just because they all fall in line with his message, we will as well. They should really give more credit to the fact we have minds of our own and will not be fed these lies."

"Yes, Ted said. So many conspiracy theories are being put out as truth and repeated to innocent citizens who truly believe them. It is so shameful to watch the falsities being spread to so many without regard for the true outcome. Our country really needs to heed a person's words and pay attention. When they hear these stories they have to check and see are there really any facts to actually support it. They have to question is it all a hoax and lies to stoke fear for no reason other than to make people believe Frump's party of soldiers can fix it? We have seen what has happened with him in charge and if there was ever a time to fear it is under his leadership not someone else's."

"I have to agree with you on that Dad said. It is his own words and rhetoric that is intentionally stoking all of us to tear each other apart when his responsibility is to bring a nation together. We have to ask ourselves how far is too far with all of this? Is it when our mother or daughter are shot and killed as innocent bystanders in a nation where carnage is so abundant? What will it take for those who look the other way to step up and take action? Ultimately, will it be too late?"

Finn was thinking this conversation seemed to be getting a bit heavy and negative. He knew just how to lighten things up.

"Alright, let's play a game. We will go around the table and come up with a Baby Frump phrase that sums up his true character."

"I already have one, Garrett said. "Total and Complete Shutdown of Muslims entering the US."

"That is one of the originals, Garrett! I have another. "I Have a Great Relationship with the Blacks."

"That goes back a way, Ted said, you gotta love how a person's words show their true intentions. "The Blacks" like they are from another world and are not part of this country, what a fool. Mine is "I take advantage of the laws of a nation. Because I am running a company."
"You took mine, Dad said. That is a good character builder! Let me think of another one. OK, got it. "We are having all of these people from shithole countries come here." Just when you think is it possible for someone to go lower. A true winner of the racism awards!"

"That was a doozy! Jean said, "I have "Any Jew voting for democrats show either a total lack of knowledge or great disloyalty." Hmmm, anti-semitic stereotype?"

"It is down to you, Mom. Finn said. What have you been waiting to tell us?"

"Mine is when he referenced four congresswomen of color, "Why don't they go back and fix the totally crime-infested places from which they came." Ummm, you mean America, you idiot?"

"Alright, Finn said, everyone picked some great quotes! Round 2 is to come up with someone that created a cover for his falsities and divisiveness."

"I must go first, his Mom said. It was all of SnellyAnne Wrongways, "Alternative Facts" comments. How do you still cover for this man, have you no shame?"

"That is a classic, Mom."

Uncle Ted chimed in with, "What about all of the voter fraud Sleazin Filler and others promoted and continues to this day?"

"Yes, Dad replied, If you can't win honestly, lie, cheat, steal, or have an adversary win the election for you. Amazing, they have never been able to offer a bit of proof to back up their lies. Oh, wait, that is because they are lies. Like, Smoug Collins, claiming the impeachment was a sham because our party lost the election. Really, Smoug? You see the evidence of his abuse, and yet that is the best you can come up with?"

"Aunt Jean said my award goes to the rally fools the supported his hateful rhetoric of congratulating a Congressman for body-slamming a reporter. There is a special place in you know where for those folks."

Garrett asked, "I am not sure if this qualifies but is it fair to call a Sharpie an accomplice if it was used to alter the truth?"
After a roaring round of laughter, the family all said, "we'll take it!"

"Wait for it, Finn said. How about this? 34 Frump peeps, three companies all charged with over 100 criminal convictions for this liar! Boom!"

"OK, we have our grand champion! "Uncle Ted said

"Thanks, Uncle, we could do this all night!"

"I am sure we could, but your Uncle and I need to hit the road. It was so nice to spend time together again and share. I just wish the country could figure out how to do this instead of being so rooted in taking sides against each other."

"I know it can happen, Garrett said. We just need someone that can lead us through it."

Finn thought he had worked so diligently on his essay assignment. Was it what he wanted to say? He felt so, but he never knew how it would be perceived. He knew he had to get used to putting words out there if this were the path he would take. Some would agree with him, and some would not. He just had to do it though. After all, it was just for his instructor and he felt solid about his class. He gave it one more glance and then with bold confidence he hit the submit button.

IMAGINE

Everyone deserves to be heard. We are all entitled to an opinion, and the uniqueness or commonality of it is what drives our passion for expressing it. As individuals, we long for our thoughts and ideas to be validated. It empowers us to make a difference, and we believe what we communicate is what people want to hear. We often seek out opinions for the direction we need when we do not have experience with different topics. Our words are powerful. They can change thinking, they can alter outcomes, they can make us feel wonderful, and often, they can hurt.

Imagine a place where you did not have to worry about what political party your neighbors affiliated with or their skin color. What if we saw them just like us as unique individuals that bring something special to us by being around them. Imagine if what we heard from our leaders could be believed, and commitments could be honored. Imagine if a person's words focused on good instead of hate, division, and blame. It is possible, but we are human. Some of us have the ability to do it while others do not. It is what it is.

In a world where opinions are often shared online and anonymously, we lose track of the effects of how impactful words are. As a reader, you do not know if I am black or white. American or Middle Eastern. Opinions carry prejudices. If I posted a picture, you would likely form specific opinions before you even started reading. Our biases are in our thoughts and often are expressed through our words. At times, what we say is what we mean, intentional or not. When we see a pattern of repeated behavior in our words, it is a telling sign of the person that exists within us. The difference lies in that what many say online, enclosed in a world of anonymity and no contact, may be far different from what they can say directly to a person's face. We have to stop and think, if I am not willing to speak this directly to a person, then should I be saying it at all?

Our country needs that leader who can speak the necessary words and not the words that divide. A person who does not see the color of our skin, and our origins, or what would be assumed to be our origins. We need to know that a person's words matter in a crisis and can be believed to be the truth and not intended to lead us astray for a self-fulfilling outcome. A person's words can cause much harm when they are false, but seen as truth. A leader we believe in that tells us to do something can be seen as valid. But if that leader is telling us to do something harmful, we still may because we put faith in that individual.

Words can cause us to stand up and take action. But the words alone do not empower us. It is within each of us to choose what we do in our response to those words. The power in words is what we make of them and not what someone tells us to do. Only you have control over yourself and you can't have power unless you know your vulnerabilities. At times, we use our word power to attempt to cover up those weaknesses. Instead, we need to be open to where we are vulnerable and we need to learn more about the why behind our concerns. Are we reacting to words out of fear or are we processing those words and making the best choice possible? Do we feel vulnerable because someone is telling us to feel that way?

Our communities are not our enemies. Our neighbors are the ones who deliver our mail, prepare our take-out, heal us when we are ill. Our neighbors support us during a disaster and donate to our cause when we do not even know it. They take care of our family at school, houses of worship, and wherever we need their assistance. To be divisive with our neighbors is like cutting off the hand that feeds you and takes care of you. Our neighbors are more than that house next door. They reach across the entire world, creating the medicines that heal us, shipping us the much-needed goods that make our lives more comfortable, cleaning our messes when we travel, and touch our lives each day in meaningful ways that we may be too blind to see. What are the words we are using when we speak of those who are there for all of us?

In the end, it is those words and actions that determine our legacy. What is it that we want to be left behind for our children, grandchildren, and family to remember? What will they be able to tell others about us? Something they are proud of or something they are too embarrassed to discuss? Was it the difference we made for all life? Or was it the battles we fought to divide our own communities because we were too caught up in words.

Each of us now has the power to determine what happens next. We have choices to make for what we want our legacy to be. This time the power of our voice is silent but resounding. It is the voice of our ballot. When we make our choice, it is quiet and unheard. But, the collective power of that quiet choice is what changes the world. We must let our voices be heard to achieve the dreams we have for ourselves and those that follow us. Take back the power that your voice matters even when others try to tell you it does not or subject to fraud. The only fraud is in the words of those trying to stop you.

REFERENCE MATERIALS

https://www.reference.com/world-view/differences-between-popular-vote-vs-electoral-vote-electoral-college-e836b6714fcb49fd

https://www.nytimes.com/2017/02/17/business/trump-calls-the-news-media-the-enemy-of-the-people.html

https://en.wikipedia.org/wiki/Timeline_of_the_Donald_Trump_presidency

https://www.politico.com/blogs/donald-trump-administration/2017/01/spicer-trump-voter-fraud-claim-234121

https://time.com/longform/donald-trump-acquitted-impeachment/
-
https://www.google.com/amp/s/www.brookings.edu/blog/fixgov/2020/03/16/trumps-failed-presidency/amp/

https://www.google.com/amp/s/www.latimes.com/politics/story/2020-06-12/republican-officials-fear-trump%3f_amp=true

https://www.google.com/amp/s/www.latimes.com/politics/story/2020-06-12/republican-officials-fear-trump%3f_amp=true

https://www.google.com/amp/s/www.washingtonpost.com/news/answer-sheet/wp/2016/11/06/the-frightening-effect-of-trump-talk-on-americas-schools/%3foutputType=amp

https://www.minnpost.com/eric-black-ink/2019/03/is-our-famous-system-of-checks-and-balances-breaking-down/

https://www.minnpost.com/eric-black-ink/2019/03/is-our-famous-system-of-checks-and-balances-breaking-down/